Who discovered
the surprising secrets
of maggots?

Biologists often had to learn by cutting open animals and finding big surprises. Here Louis Pasteur (1822–1895) cuts open a piglet in his study of measles.

Who showed that
something as simple as
having a drink of
water could kill?

People often thought that biologists were a bit strange, as they secretly worked in their **laboratories** with live creatures, bottles of blood or dead bodies. But was the world of bizarre biology really like this? You may be surprised to find out just how weird the history of science could be…

Who changed a pig's
nose from pink
to green?

# In the beginning

Just imagine how the first people on Earth tried to make sense of everyday life. There are so many questions. What makes grass grow? What are seeds? Why do we have to eat? Why do we get ill? To find answers, people had to try things out. As they began to grow plants for food and keep animals, they found answers to some of these questions. But many mysteries remained.

About 5,000 years ago the ancient Egyptians were probably the first people to mix flour and water with tiny living things called **yeasts**. This simple biology made their bread rise, giving it the spongy texture that bread has today.

## Did you know?

When people first cooked and baked food, they used simple science. Cooking plants and meat made the food easier to digest. More than 10,000 years ago people first mixed flour with water and baked a type of flat bread. About 5,000 years later they discovered yeast could make the dough rise into soft spongy bread.

Ancient Egyptians stopped dead bodies from rotting as they believed this kept the person's spirit intact. ••••◦

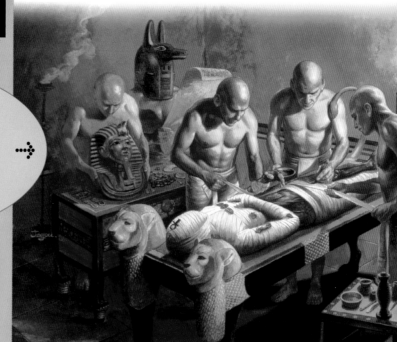

yeasts  microbes called fungi that help to make some foods

# A Weird History of Science

# Bizarre Biology

## John Townsend

Raintree

## www.raintreepublishers.co.uk
Visit our website to find out more information about **Raintree** books.

To order:
- ☎ Phone 44 (0) 1865 888112
- 🖹 Send a fax to 44 (0) 1865 314091
- 💻 Visit the Raintree bookshop at **www.raintreepublishers.co.uk** to browse our catalogue and order online.

MONKEY PUZZLE MEDIA LTD

Produced for Raintree by
Monkey Puzzle Media Ltd
Gissing's Farm, Fressingfield
Suffolk IP21 5SH, UK

First published in Great Britain by Raintree,
Halley Court, Jordan Hill, Oxford OX2 8EJ,
part of Harcourt Education.
Raintree is a registered trademark
of Harcourt Education Ltd.

Editor: Steve Parker
Designer: Tim Mayer
Picture Researcher: Lynda Lines
Production: Chloe Bloom
Originated by Modern Age
Printed and bound in China
by South China Printing Company

ISBN 978 1 4062 0556 5 (hardback)
11 10 09 08 07
10 9 8 7 6 5 4 3 2 1

ISBN 978 1 4062 0561 9 (paperback)
12 11 10 09 08
10 9 8 7 6 5 4 3 2 1

**British Library Cataloguing in
Publication Data**
Townsend, John, 1955–
Bizarre biology. – (A weird history of science)
1.Biology – History – Juvenile literature
I.Title
570.9

**Acknowledgements**
Columbia University p. **38** (Graduate School of
Journalism); Corbis pp. **4** (Bettmann), **5 bottom**
(Eddie Cheng/EPA), **8**, **14** (Bettmann), **23**
(Hulton-Deutsch Collection), **32**, **40** (Theo
Allofs), **44** (Eddie Cheng/EPA), **45** (Reuters), **46**
(Peter Schouten/National Geographic Society),
**47** (EPA), **48** (Jonathan Blair); Getty Images pp.
**7** (National Geographic), **13** (PhotoDisc), **17**
(PhotoDisc), **25** (Time Life Pictures), **27**, **29**, **43**
(PhotoDisc), **49** (AFP); Mary Evans Picture
Library pp. **5 middle**, **16**, **20**, **28**, **36**; Rex
Features p. **37** (Michael Burke); Science Photo
Library pp. **1** (Jean-Loup Charmet), **5 top right**
(Volker Steger), **6** (Christian Jegou, Publiphoto
Diffusion), **11** (Jean-Loup Charmet), **15** (Volker
Steger), **21** (Dr. Gopal Murti), **22** (St. Mary's
Hospital Medical School), **24** (Sheila Terry), **26**,
**31** (Dr. Keith Roberts/Kim Findlay), **33** (Jean-
Loup Charmet), **34** (James King-Holmes), **35**
(John Reader), **39** (Tom McHugh), **41** (Peter
Scoones); Topfoto.co.uk pp. **5 top**, **9**, **10**, **12**,
**18**, **19** (Sean Sprague/Images Works), **30**, **42**.

Cover photograph of a volunteer testing a
military respirator reproduced with permission
of Getty Images.

Every effort has been made to contact copyright
holders of any material reproduced in this book.
Any omissions will be rectified in subsequent
printings if notice is given to the publishers.

**Disclaimer**
All the Internet addresses (URLs) given in this
book were valid at the time of going to press.
However, due to the dynamic nature of the
Internet, some addresses may have changed, or
sites may have changed or ceased to exist since
publication. While the author and publishers
regret any inconvenience this may cause readers,
no responsibility for any such changes can be
accepted by either the author or the publishers.

# Contents

Any words appearing in the text in bold,
**like this**, are explained in the glossary.
You can also look out for them in the "Word
bank" at the bottom of each page.

# Risky business

**Did you know?**

The word "biology" comes from the Greek words bio and logi-, which mean "the study of life". So biology is about trying to understand all living things, from the tiniest **microbes** to huge plants like trees, also animals of all kinds – and humans.

Science has always been full of risks. Being a scientist and finding out about "the unknown" can bring scary surprises. Handling substances that can poison, explode or cause disease are just some of the dangers. Scientists ask questions such as "What makes things happen?" – and risk getting the answers wrong. For people working in medicine, such mistakes can be a matter of life and death.

Modern science takes great care. But long ago many scientists had to learn the hard way. Much of what we know today came from people in the past taking risks and learning from their mistakes.

## The science of life

Biology is the science of life. It involves the study of animals and plants, living and dead. It also studies human life and has led to all kinds of medical developments. In the search for knowledge, biologists have sometimes taken great risks with their own lives and those of others.

In the 1730s Stephen Hales studied the blood pressure of animals. He connected a glass tube to a horse's artery and measured how high the blood spurted inside the tube.

**Word bank**

laboratory  scientific work place for experiments, called a "lab"
microbes  tiny living things only seen with a microscope

## Stopping the rot

The ancient Egyptians knew about the biology of rotting or decay. They learned how to stop dead bodies rotting away by wrapping them up as mummies. They believed this would keep dead people safe in the "after-life".

The Egyptians didn't know that **microbes** caused rotting. But they knew that sealing bodies with bandages, beeswax, sugar gum, and plant oils would keep out air and water, and so stop the rot. This preserved the bodies for thousands of years. For the Egyptians, biology was not just the science of life, but also the science of death.

### Keeping fresh

Ancient Egyptians found a way to stop dead bodies rotting from the inside, as well as from the outside. They dried them out. First they took out the inner parts such as the liver, stomach, and lungs. Then they wrapped up the body as a mummy. This simple biology made sure dead Egyptians lasted a very long time.

This Ancient Egyptian mummy of the ruler Merenptah is more than 3,200 years old.

7

## Greek and Roman discoveries

Aristotle was a scientist in Greece about 2,300 years ago. He asked all kinds of questions like: "Why do chickens lay eggs?" He cut open eggs to study the growing chicks inside. He also studied bees and how they make honey.

Although Aristotle began to understand how parts of the human body work, some of his ideas turned out to be wrong. He thought the heart was where we think and feel emotions. He thought the brain was for cooling the blood. One of his strange ideas was to rub goat's **urine** into his head to cure his baldness. He thought this would feed his scalp – but it didn't work!

### Hit and miss

For thousands of years people thought magical powers or curses made them ill. They tried cures such as making spells or pleasing the gods. They often used plants to make medicines. The Romans and Greeks knew the plant **mandrake** was poisonous. But they put small amounts of it into wine to help patients sleep. It was risky science.

Aristotle studied many animals and recorded everything he saw.

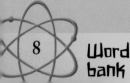

**Word bank**

arteries  tubes that carry blood from the heart around the body
bacteria  microbes that live everywhere, some causing disease

# Heart and blood

Galen was a doctor in Rome more than 1,800 years ago. He cut open the bodies of apes and pigs so he could understand how human bodies worked. At that time doctors thought the tubes called **arteries** carried air round the body. Galen proved that they carried blood, which was pumped by the heart. Even though he did not know that blood goes round and round the body in a constant flow, Galen's discoveries were big steps in science. Many of his notes still survive today. They affected the study of medicine for hundreds of years.

Claudius Galen (AD 129–216) was the greatest medical scientist of Roman times.

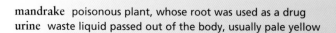

mandrake  poisonous plant, whose root was used as a drug
urine  waste liquid passed out of the body, usually pale yellow

## Medieval medicine

The years from about AD 600 to AD 1500 in Europe are known as medieval times. Blood in those days was something of a puzzle. People knew it was needed to keep bodies alive, but what did it do? Medieval scientists did not have microscopes to study blood closely. They had no idea that blood was so special.

Cutting open bodies to look at organs and muscles helped Leonardo da Vinci understand human biology and make detailed drawings like this.

# Bleeding

Like the ancient Greeks, people in medieval times often made themselves bleed on purpose. This was called **blood letting**, done because people thought too much blood was bad for them. They sometimes went to a barber to be "bled" or they put leeches on their skin. Leeches drank their blood and were thought to suck out disease or bad feelings.

People thought that a person's mood was caused by too many "fluids" in the body. There were four main fluids. **Phlegm** made you sluggish and dull. Yellow **bile** made you angry quickly. Black bile made you gloomy and sad. Blood made you extremely happy!

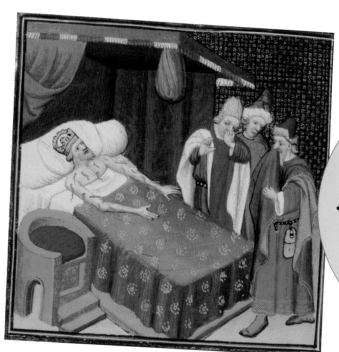

A book from the 1300s showed how doctors covered a patient's body with leeches. His disease made him smell so much that the doctors kept their distance.

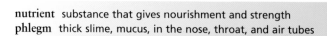

nutrient  substance that gives nourishment and strength
phlegm  thick slime, mucus, in the nose, throat, and air tubes

# Disgusting discoveries

Finding out how living things worked often led scientists to try out some crazy ideas. Sometimes these led to discoveries that were amazing ... or just horribly disgusting.

## Chilling the blood

Francis Bacon was an English writer with a great interest in science – but it turned out to be the death of him. One snowy day in 1625, Bacon wondered if snow could preserve meat. There were no freezers then, and meat soon rotted if it wasn't treated with salt. To test his idea, Bacon took a dead chicken outside and stuffed it full of snow to freeze it. The chicken didn't freeze, but Bacon did. He died shortly after, from **pneumonia**.

## New methods

At one time very few biologists kept written records. In the 1600s, William Harvey kept a fact book. He wrote in it only after his ideas were carefully tested. He cut up bodies, made careful notes, and rubbed out anything that did not pass a re-test. Soon all biologists began to work in this detailed way.

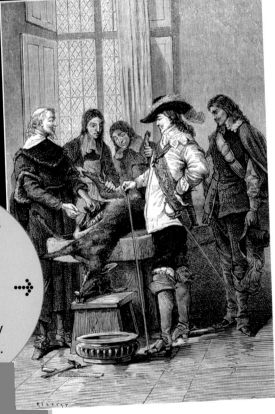

William Harvey showed King Charles I and doctors how blood flowed round the body of a living deer.

pneumonia  lung disease causing fever, cough, and wheezing

# Biology breakthrough

William Harvey (1578–1657) was a London doctor who had a new way of working. He cut up dead animals – from dogs and pigs to slugs and oysters. He gave lectures about what he found inside them. In 1628 he wrote a book which was a great breakthrough in human biology. He described how the heart did not make blood flow to and fro. Instead, the heart was a muscle that pumped the blood round and round the body, called the circulation. Many doctors called Harvey "bizarre", but before long they agreed he was right.

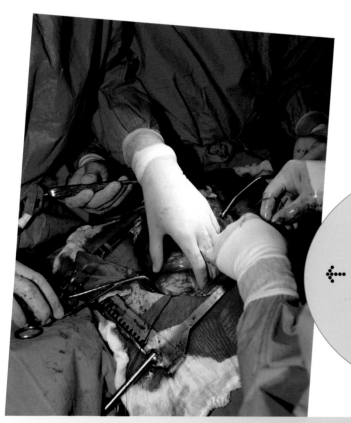

## Can you believe it?

In 1667 French scientist Jean-Baptiste Denis injected a sick man with lamb's blood to make him better. This was the first recorded blood **transfusion** to a human. The man "recovered, grew fatter, and was a surprise to all who knew him". But this was dangerous. Animal blood is very different from human blood and many of Denis's other patients died from this type of transfusion.

As scientists learned more about the heart, it eventually became possible to remove a patient's diseased heart and replace it with a healthy one from a donor.

**transfusion**  putting fluid, such as blood, from one body into another

## Maggot mysteries

What happens if you leave out an old piece of meat to rot? Soon it's full of maggots. Where do they come from? Scientists in the 17th century believed that maggots just grew out of the dead meat.

Francesco Redi (1626–1697) was an Italian scientist who carried out a famous experiment in 1668. He took three jars and put meat in each. He tightly sealed one, left one open, and covered the third with **gauze**. Can you guess what happened?

Maggots appeared on the meat in the open jar, but not in the sealed one. Maggots also appeared on the gauze cover of the third jar. Redi had shown that live maggots did not form inside rotting meat, but came from eggs laid by flies. The maggots appeared on the gauze because flies were attracted to the meat beneath but could not get to it.

## Did you know?

Maggots were a puzzle for hundreds of years, seeming to appear from nowhere. We now know they are the grubs or **larvae** of flies. Each female fly can lay up to 500 eggs, often in meat. The maggots hatch from the eggs within a day and feed on the meat, helping it to rot.

Before Francisco Redi did his experiments, everyone believed insect life could develop out of nowhere: lice from sweaty clothes, beetles from rotting wood, horseflies from manure, and maggots from rotting meat.

**Word bank**

gauze woven fabric of fine material or wires

## Buzzing with new biology

Redi found that when he put dead flies or dead maggots in sealed jars with meat, no live maggots appeared. When he did the same with living flies, maggots did appear. He also found that maggots turned into flies – which no one knew before. These were big discoveries for the world of biology.

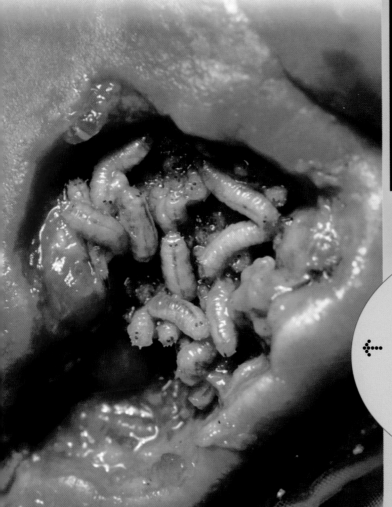

Maggots eat away dead flesh in wounds but leave healthy areas alone. They are sometimes used by doctors to clean out infected wounds.

**larvae** young, wingless, wormlike grubs

## Tiny life

Have you cleaned your teeth today? The **microbes** called **bacteria** in your mouth can make teeth rot away. More than 300 years ago a Dutch scientist first saw how "tiny animals" lived inside people's mouths.

In 1683 Anton van Leeuwenhoek made some of the most important discoveries in the history of biology. He discovered such things as bacteria and blood **cells**. That was because he made an early type of simple microscope, using a single powerful lens that could magnify over 200 times. In fact, Leeuwenhoek made more than 500 microscopes. He was the first person to see clear images of microscopic life – on teeth.

Anton van Leeuwenhoek was amazed to discover living microbes, which he called "animalcules".

**Word bank**   cell  microscopic part or "building block" of a living thing

## Slimy teeth

One of the substances that Leeuwenhoek examined under his microscope was the slimy **plaque** between his teeth. He called it "white matter, thick as batter". He described how he saw "many very little living animals moving". He was looking at the bacteria which live inside mouths. Then he looked at plaque from old people who had never cleaned their teeth. He was in for a shock. Under his microscope, Leeuwenhoek saw "an unbelievably great company of living animals swimming more nimbly than any I had ever seen up to this time". The bacteria were not only alive but very active!

## Itching to discover more

Anton van Leeuwenhoek was the first biologist to watch the tiny development of the flea. He saw how it hatched from an egg and grew into an adult. This was the first time that the tiniest living things were seen to have a life cycle and even body parts inside them, like any larger creature.

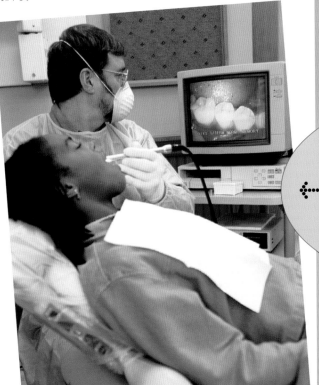

Dentists today use advanced ways of checking for microbes and plaque that can cause tooth decay.

plaque  sticky film of old food and bacteria on teeth

## Dangerous germs

Some 200 years after scientists first saw **bacteria** under a microscope, they still had no idea how they lived. French biologist Louis Pasteur realized that these tiny **microbes** could get into our bodies and even kill us.

Louis Pasteur's idea that microbes could cause illness – the "germ **theory** of disease" – seemed bizarre at the time. He knew bacteria lived in soil, water, and air, and on plants and animals. He was also sure that they could get into our mouths and make us ill. They could also get into people's bodies through cuts, scratches, and bites – even those which were too small to see or feel.

Louis Pasteur took a great risk when he first injected Joseph with rabies cells.

**Word bank**

rabies  deadly disease of the nerves and brain
theory  general idea to explain how something happens

Today vaccines are given all round the world to protect people against diseases that used to kill millions.

# Big risk

In 1885, a woman took her nine-year-old son Joseph to see Pasteur. Joseph had been bitten by a dog with the terrible disease of **rabies**. Joseph would catch it and die without help.

Pasteur kept body parts of animals in his lab, including the nerves of rabbits that had died of rabies. It was a big risk, but he injected Joseph with a fluid called a **vaccine**, made from these nerves. Joseph had one injection each day for two weeks, in an attempt to protect him against the disease.

The vaccine worked. Joseph did not catch rabies. It was a great breakthrough in the treatment of this dreaded disease.

## Saving lives worldwide

Injecting people with vaccines was once thought to be ridiculous. Today millions of people have vaccines to protect them from dangerous diseases. A vaccine is made from dead or weakened microbes that cannot cause disease, but which make the body build up resistance or immunity.

vaccine   dead or weakened microbes which make the body resistant to a disease

## Drinking cholera

For hundreds of years cholera was one of the world's big killer diseases. No one knew how people caught it until John Snow, a British doctor, proved that the disease was spread in dirty water. He found that a London cholera **epidemic** in the 1850s started where sewage got into the water supply.

Other scientists, like Louis Pasteur, were also sure **bacteria** in dirty water caused diseases. Yet many people still drank from rivers where they put their toilet waste. No wonder cholera and other illnesses spread quickly. In 1883 a German scientist, Robert Koch, at last discovered the exact bacteria that caused the disease. This was the first example of a **microbe** being linked to a disease.

### Fast facts on cholera

Cholera is a deadly disease that spreads quickly when people drink the bacteria in dirty water. Victims become ill with severe **diarrhoea** and **vomiting**. Losing fluids so suddenly from the body can lead to death if the patient does not keep drinking clean water. Today cholera can be treated with medical drugs.

Cartoons in the 1860s showed how water from a pump in London could be deadly to anyone who dared to drink it.

20

**Word bank**

diarrhoea  runny bowel motions (excrement)
epidemic  when a disease spreads quickly over a wide area

## Don't try this!

Max von Pettenkofer was a German scientist who didn't agree that bacteria in water spread disease. He said that "bad air" caused most kinds of illnesses. He felt so strongly about this that he set out to prove Koch was wrong about cholera. But what Pettenkofer did was very dangerous indeed.

In 1892 Pettenkofer drank a test tube of foul water crammed with cholera bacteria! He wanted to show that bacteria alone did not cause the disease. The next day he felt fine, and spoke to news reporters who had expected to find him dead. Three days later he became mildly ill but amazingly he survived his unwise experiment. No one knew how he had survived – but he had been very lucky.

### The end of a career

Von Pettenkofer's bizarre biology experiment was laughed at by other scientists. Before long, they all knew that bacteria in water caused cholera and Pettenkofer had taken an unnecessary risk. No one took him seriously any more. He became very unhappy, and in 1901 he killed himself.

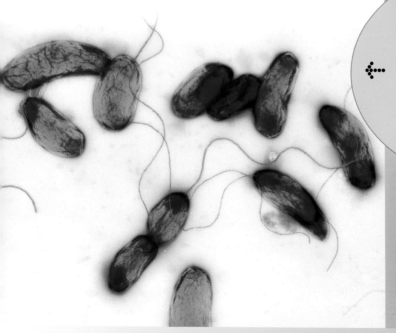

Water might look clean but it could contain deadly cholera bacteria like this that can only be seen with a microscope.

## Medicines from mould

In 1928 British scientist Alexander Fleming (1881–1955) made a great discovery by mistake – all because he was untidy. Fleming was working on **bacteria** in London before he went away on holiday. He left the lid off a dish of bacteria on his lab bench. This let tiny seed-like **spores** of moulds, which drift in the air, land on the dish … where they began to grow. When Fleming came back two weeks later he was amazed to see mould growing in the dish. Even more astonishing, the mould had killed the bacteria that had been in the dish.

Alexander Fleming made his amazing discovery at his desk in London, England.

**Word bank**

antibiotic substance that kills harmful bacteria
fungi living things that feed on dead or rotting material

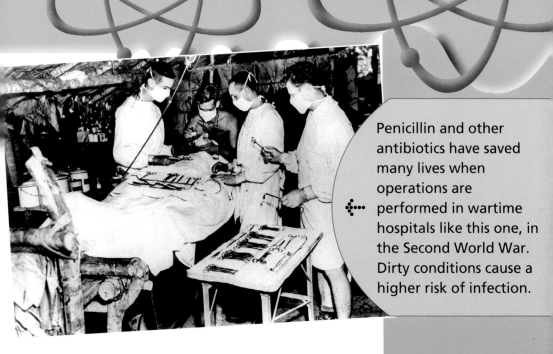

Penicillin and other antibiotics have saved many lives when operations are performed in wartime hospitals like this one, in the Second World War. Dirty conditions cause a higher risk of infection.

## Breaking the mould

Fleming was stunned. He had found something called an **antibiotic**, that attacked and killed harmful disease-spreading bacteria. The mould was called penicillium. Fleming realized the substance it made, which he named penicillin, might become a medical drug used to treat diseases and infections.

## Bottles and bedpans

It took many years to make enough penicillin to test properly. Howard Florey (1898–1968) was an Australian scientist working in England. In 1940, he and his team found that penicillin was powerful at fighting all kinds of diseases. They grew the mould in milk churns, lemonade bottles, and bedpans. Then they injected penicillin into patients whose blood had been poisoned with bacteria. Penicillin made them better.

### Proof that mould saves lives

In 1940 Howard Florey's team did one of the most important medical experiments in history. They injected eight mice with deadly bacteria. Four of the mice were then treated with penicillin. The next day, the treated mice had recovered but the untreated mice were dead. The new wonder-drug passed the test.

spore  tiny seed that can grow into a new mould or fungus

# Dangerous experiments

Joseph Priestley (1733–1804) did experiments with burning candles and mice, noting how mice had to have oxygen to stay alive. He was one of the first scientists to study the process called **respiration.** He also put shoots of plants into a container of water, then covered it over, leaving a lit candle inside. Surprisingly the candle stayed alight. It did not go out because its burning had used up the oxygen in the air. This was because more oxygen was produced by the plant, by the process known as **photosynthesis.**

Joseph Wright's famous painting, *An Experiment on a Bird in the Air Pump.*

Word bank

photosynthesis  when plants use light energy to make their own food, giving off oxygen in the process

## Twitching

During the 1780s Italian biologist Luigi Galvani experimented with frogs and electricity. He found that electricity could make a frog's leg jump – even when it was no longer attached to the frog! While cutting a frog leg, Galvani's steel knife touched a brass hook holding the leg in place. The leg twitched. Galvani thought he was seeing "animal electricity" – a life force within the muscles of the frog. In fact he had unknowingly made electricity by touching various metals and substances together. The electricity passed through the frog's leg muscles and made it kick.

### Just so you know

Luigi Galvani's name is remembered in various ways. The word "galvanize" means to leap into sudden action. It also means using electricity to coat an object with the anti-rust metal zinc. And a galvanometer measures electricity.

### Tests on animals

Animals were once used in all kinds of experiments which we would now think were cruel. But in the 1700s most scientists believed that animals could not think or feel pain. Today there are much stricter rules about the use of animals in experiments.

Galvani was amazed to see frogs' legs move when he touched them with an electrical machine.

respiration  when living things take in oxygen and release carbon dioxide

## Gross methods

Have you ever wondered what happens to the food you eat? The Italian scientist Lazzaro Spallanzani (1729–1799) tried to find out the fate of the food he swallowed.

In the 1700s very little was known about the digestion of food inside the body. Some scientists thought the stomach just churned up food into little bits. Others thought there was a sort of bubbly chemical reaction. Another idea was that food simply rotted as it went through the body. There was no way of telling. So Spallanzani decided to experiment – first on animals, and then on himself.

## Swallowed whole

Spallanzani put some bread in a linen bag, sewed it up, and swallowed it. About 23 hours later the results came out, when he went to the toilet! The bag and thread were intact, but the bread had disappeared. Next Spallanzani gulped down four grapes without chewing them. They all came out whole after a day. The human digestive system was clearly not a grinding machine.

## Crazy science

In the late 1700s Lazzaro Spallanzani fed birds with food inside bags on long pieces of string. After a while he pulled the string to bring the bags back up from their stomachs. From his results, Spallanzani found that a major part of digestion is the action of fluids in the stomach. Spallanzani named these fluids **gastric juice**.

Lazzaro Spallanzani experimented on birds to see how they digested food.

**Word bank**

gastric juice powerful liquid made in the stomach wall to help digestion

Next Spallanzani filled a small wooden tube with chewed meat, put it in a linen bag and swallowed the lot. He reported that the bag and tube came out empty after 22 hours. It seemed that his digestive juices had worked without any squeezing and grinding.

Spallanzani would be amazed at X-ray machines like this 1915 version, which can see inside the body. But the dangers of X-rays were not understood at first. Today these people watching would be behind X-ray-proof screens.

## Dabbling with death

Throughout history, smallpox was a dreaded disease. In the 1700s it killed millions of people every year, including about a third of the children who caught it. Their skin became covered in blisters filled with **pus**. Those who survived could be left blind or with terrible scars called **pockmarks**. There was no cure.

The strange thing was that people who milked cows often caught a mild form of smallpox and then recovered. They probably first caught the germs from cows, so it was called cowpox. Even stranger, no one who caught cowpox ever went on to catch smallpox. A British doctor, Edward Jenner, wondered why. Then he did something scary – twice.

A cartoon from 1802 shows how people might begin to change into cows after vaccination with cowpox pus.

**Word bank**

pockmark  round scar left on the skin after a spot or blister
pus  thick yellow or green liquid caused by infection

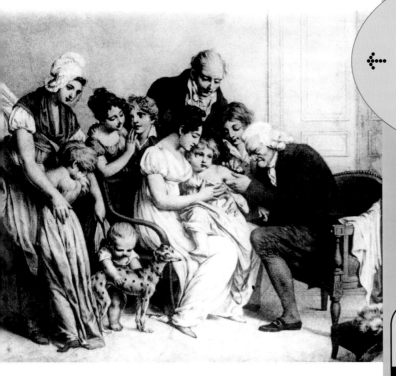

The story of Edward Jenner and the first smallpox vaccine was shown in many paintings in the 1800s.

## Big risk

In 1796 Jenner asked his gardener to lend his young son for an experiment. First, eight-year-old James Phipps agreed to be injected with pus taken from a cowpox blister on the hand of a milkmaid. Second, and even riskier, Jenner injected James with deadly smallpox. If James caught the disease, he would probably die. It was a daring experiment but James did not catch smallpox. Jenner proved that people could be protected against the disease. It was a major breakthrough in the history of medical science. Later other scientists such as Louis Pasteur carried on the work.

## Can you believe it?

Nearly 200 years after Jenner's scary experiment, smallpox was finally beaten. In 1980, it was the first human disease to be totally wiped out, throughout the world. And it all began with Edward Jenner and brave James Phipps. A few samples of the smallpox germ or **virus** are still kept in labs, just in case it appears again.

**virus** tiniest kind of disease-causing microbe

# Causing a stir

Clergyman and scientist John Needham (1713–1781) made soup which seemed to produce tiny living things out of nowhere, even after being boiled. He believed the fluid itself made life. In fact, it was **bacteria** in his soup. He hadn't boiled it enough or there were bacteria already on the pans he used.

Life has always been seen as very special. When biologists "messed with life" and appeared to "play at being God", many people became upset and some turned angry.

## Where does life begin?

Most people used to base their beliefs on what they saw around them, without really testing their ideas. If young frogs hopped out of mud, it was assumed the mud itself created them. Some scientists in the 18th century believed insects could emerge from any substance at all. They believed in a "life force" in all matter. Living things could appear from almost anything. It was known as spontaneous generation.

## Messing with nature

Andrew Crosse claimed he created life itself. He lived in a country house with its own lab. Wires to the roof crackled during his experiments in thunderstorms. In 1836 he passed electricity through a dish of chemicals – and made "a perfect insect". Crosse was sure he had created animals: "As they burst into life, the table was covered with similar insects".

 Andrew Crosse (1784–1855) was fascinated by electricity.

**Word bank**  blight  plant disease caused by fungi or insects

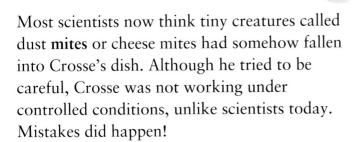

Most scientists now think tiny creatures called dust **mites** or cheese mites had somehow fallen into Crosse's dish. Although he tried to be careful, Crosse was not working under controlled conditions, unlike scientists today. Mistakes did happen!

## Angry neighbours

Andrew Crosse got into big trouble when he told people he had created insect life in his lab. His claims upset many people who said he was messing with nature and trying to be God. Farmers threatened to attack him for causing a disease called **blight** on their wheat crops. Crosse stopped his work and decided it was safer to keep quiet.

Cheese mites were the most likely culprits of Crosse's experiment as they had probably found their way into his mixture. Mites are usually smaller than this full stop.

**mites** tiny spider-like animals that live on plants, animals and stored foods

## Shocking new ideas

Some biologists asked big questions about humans and animals – where they came from, and if they might be related. But they faced great opposition. Many people thought such questions were more to do with religion than science.

Scientists had long tried to understand how different kinds, or species, of animals and plants seemed suited or adapted to their surroundings. Why were some better at surviving than others? And had humans changed over thousands of years? These were difficult questions. Some church leaders became furious with biologists who even dared to suggest that humans may have once come from animals like apes.

Lamarck believed that if a giraffe stretched its neck longer during its life, it would have longer-necked offspring. But neck length depends on **genes**.

**Word bank**

evolution  when plants and animals alter gradually from parents to offspring over a very long time

# Wild ideas

Charles Darwin (1809–1882) was a British biologist who developed ideas about **evolution**. He spent years studying different animals all around the world. He noted how some species seemed to adapt and change over time. Could one species develop into another with very small, step-by-step changes, passed from parents to offspring, over a very long time?

Darwin had these ideas more than 20 years before he dared to publish them in 1859. His book *The Origin of the Species* caused a storm. Some people thought he was attacking the Bible. When he later suggested that human beings had evolved from apes, he was mocked and many people hated his ideas.

Charles Darwin was often shown as half-human, half-monkey, because of his ideas about evolution.

**genes** instructions for features (like eye colour), which are passed from parents to offspring

## Scandals in biology

Gregor Mendel was an Austrian monk who bred almost 30,000 pea plants from 1858 to 1866, and recorded all the details. He bred together different types of peas and noted which features of the parent plants passed to the offspring.

At the time, scientists took little notice of Mendel's work. But by 1900 they realized its true value. Some made a fuss by suggesting he cheated. However, Mendel is now considered the founder of the area of biology called **genetics** (see pages 42–43).

### No fuss

Unlike Charles Darwin, Gregor Mendel (1822–1884) failed to cause a stir while he was alive. In fact, he wished other scientists would take even a slight interest in his efforts: "I am convinced that it will not be long before the whole world acknowledges the results of my work." He was right, unfortunately it was not in his lifetime.

Gregor Mendel and his study of pea plants ⋯➔ began important discoveries about genes.

  **Word bank**

genetics  branch of biology that deals with how features are passed on, or inherited, from parents to offspring

## Discovery of the century

Twenty years after Darwin's death, another storm about **evolution** hit the science world. In 1912 an ancient skull, dug up at Piltdown in Sussex, England, was said to be a link between apes and humans. Biologists all over the world were excited by the amazing discovery. It was just what they had been looking for. The skull was like a human's, but the jaw was more like an ape's.

For many years the half-human, half-ape "Piltdown Man" seemed proof of Darwin's **theory** of evolution. But then came the bombshell. In 1953 new scientific tests showed that the skull was from a human, but not from very long ago. And the jaw came from a real ape, an orang-utan. Piltdown Man was a hoax. The science world had been tricked for 40 years!

## Just a fraud

In the 1950s a new chemical test could tell the age of bone remains. Scientists checked Piltdown Man. Instead of being millions of years old, the jaw turned out to be 600 years old. An unknown joker had cleverly put together a human skull and an ape's jaw, stained so they seemed to belong together. Oops!

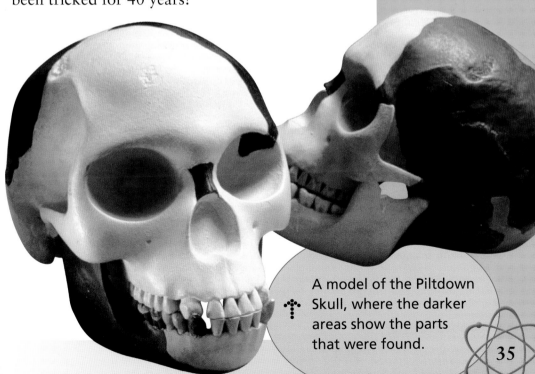

A model of the Piltdown Skull, where the darker areas show the parts that were found.

## Funny bones

It wasn't so long ago that some scientists were laughed at for suggesting huge animals once walked the Earth. The very idea of enormous lizards or flying, dragon-like creatures seemed bizarre. But through the 19th century scientists began to dig up strange bone-shaped bits of rock that made them ask many questions. Did these come from weird beasts? If so, where had they come from and what happened to them all?

Just over 150 years ago, people had no idea about how old Earth really was. Fossils were also a mystery. Were they the remains of real animals and plants, or just strange-shaped pieces of rock?

### Just so you know

Fossils are remains from past life on Earth, such as bones, teeth, shells, leaves, trees, tracks, and burrows. Scientists who study fossils and ancient forms of life are called palaeontologists.

At first, many people refused to believe that dinosaurs had ever existed. This cartoon shows Robert Owen trying to ride one of his dinosaurs.

Diplodocus  huge plant-eating dinosaur from 140 million years ago

Pterosaurs or "winged lizards", are often called pterodactyls. They lived from about 228 million to 65 million years ago.

## Fighting over fossils

Separate bits of broken fossils didn't make much sense until the first almost complete dinosaur skeleton was found, in 1858 in New Jersey, USA. It was a **Hadrosaurus**. The discovery amazed scientists and there was a sudden rush to uncover more remains. In fact there was a fierce race, called the "Bone Wars". American scientists tried to beat each other in finding the next dinosaur skeleton. They raided each other's fossil-collecting camps, smashed valuable finds and even stole fossils from their rivals.

## Big finds

In 1870, Othniel Charles Marsh discovered the first North American fossils of a **pterosaur** or flying reptile, in Kansas. He worked out its wingspan as about seven metres (23 feet). In 1877 fossils from one of the longest dinosaurs, **Diplodocus**, were found at Como Bluff, Wyoming. It was about 27 metres (90 feet) in length.

Hadrosaurus  duck-billed, plant-eating dinosaur from 80 million years ago
pterosaur  extinct flying reptile with large wings

# Bizarre beyond belief

## Hybrids

In biology a **hybrid** is the offspring of two different species, such as a zebra and a donkey. Humans have managed to **crossbreed** these particular animals and called the offspring a zedonk. The oldest word for the offspring was "zebroid" in 1899, followed by "zebrule" in 1903. Such hybrids can be seen today in some zoos.

Not all animals today are as nature intended. Humans have bred some species over many years and totally changed them. About 12,000 years ago people first started keeping wolves as pets. They began to "interfere with biology" by choosing which wolves should have cubs, known as selective breeding.

Today's 400 dog breeds have all come from those original wolves by selective breeding. Yet many "designer dogs" seem nothing like their wolf **ancestors**.

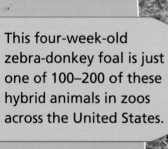

This four-week-old zebra-donkey foal is just one of 100–200 of these hybrid animals in zoos across the United States.

**Word bank**

ancestor  orginal living thing from which others are descended
crossbreed  breed together two varieties or species

# A freak of nature?

Some animals appear to be strange mixtures of different creatures. The duck-billed platypus of Australia is a mammal like a beaver, but it lays eggs and has a beak like a bird! It is such an unusual animal that when Europeans first saw a stuffed one in 1797, they thought different animals had been sewn together as a joke. Scientist Everard Jones studied a platypus in 1802 and showed that it really did exist.

The duck-billed platypus was once thought to be a freak of nature.

## Can you believe it?

A tigon is a cross between a male tiger and a female lion. A liger is the opposite. These hybrids were known in zoos in the 19th century. They do not occur naturally in the wild, as lions and tigers have very different behaviour and **habitats**. Tigers have also been bred with female ligers to produce ti-ligers.

## Just so you know

The name "platypus" means "flat-footed". The platypus is not actually flat-footed but its webbed feet make it appear so. It is one of only four kinds of mammal that lay eggs. The other three are types of echidnas, also called spiny anteaters.

habitat   natural environment or home of an animal or plant
hybrid   offspring of two different species or varieties

## Weird creatures

In the last 100 years biologists have discovered more about animal life than ever before. They have found many new species they never knew existed. Some were particularly surprising.

## Dragon found

Can you believe that scientists knew nothing about the largest lizard on Earth until 1912? It is the Komodo dragon, and its discovery was a major scientific find. The Komodo dragon is the largest **predator** on the islands where it lives, in Indonesia. It can even hunt and kill a large water buffalo, as well as a human! Scientists have studied deadly **bacteria** in the Komodo dragon's mouth. These bacteria quickly infect and poison anything it bites.

## A scary discovery

In 1912 a pilot was in a plane crash in the sea near Indonesia. He swam ashore and was shocked to see giant monsters like dinosaurs on the beach. Luckily, he was able to radio for help. When he told rescuers about the giant reptiles that lived on the island, no one believed him. In fact, he had discovered Komodo dragons.

A Komodo dragon walks along the beach on Komodo Island, Indonesia. It flicks out its tongue to smell where food might be.

**Word bank**  extinct  no longer existing or active

## Fossil fish

Discovering such a large animal in the last century was remarkable enough. But then came another amazing find. This was an ancient fish that scientists had only ever studied as a fossil, from the age of the dinosaurs. But in 1938 the fish appeared alive and well in the Indian Ocean near Africa. It was a coelacanth. Biologists thought this fish had been **extinct** for 70 million years. More of these ancient fish have been found since – sometimes on slabs at the fish market!

Fishermen in the Indian Ocean were surprised to catch a rare and strange coelacanth fish.

predator animal that kills and eats other animals

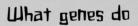

## What genes do

Genes are messages stored inside nearly every cell in the body. They tell cells what to do, so the body keeps working properly. Scientists try to understand the genetic messages that mean some people respond to medicines in an unusual way, or are more likely to develop certain diseases than other people.

# Controlling nature

Is it right to control nature? Biologists can now take microscopic **cells** from plants and animals to "grow" new living things in test tubes. They have made new copies of an original plant or animal with exactly the same **genes**. The copies are called **clones**.

In Scotland in 1996 a sheep called Dolly was the first mammal to be cloned from another adult mammal. The world was stunned that a copy of a sheep could be developed in a **laboratory**. Cloning was done using microscopic needles to move the **genetic** material, called DNA.

Professor Ian Wilmut led the team that created Dolly the cloned sheep.

## Just so you know

Every plant, animal, and human has genes made of DNA (deoxyribonucleic acid). They are in every cell of the body. If you think of yourself as this book, the words are like your genes and each letter is like your DNA. When they all come together in the right pattern they make something amazing – you!

**Word bank**

clone  living thing that has the same genes as another
embryo  living thing in the very early stages of development

# Mind-boggling

Dolly began as a tiny **embryo** in a dish. As she developed she was put into the womb of another sheep and born normally. Dolly lived to be just six years old. Some scientists think cloned animals may die younger than normal animals.

In 2003 scientists from many countries finished the first part of a huge project to "map" all the genes in our own DNA. This complete list of all the chemical parts of human DNA is called the human genome.

For years gardeners have been "controlling nature" by developing plants and flowers, such as rose breeds that do not occur in the wild.

# Yesterday, today, and tomorrow

What was once thought to be bizarre science fiction sometimes becomes science fact.

In 1997 Jay Vacanti at the University of Massachusetts, USA grew a human ear from **cells** put into a moulded shape on the back of a mouse. This caused outrage among animal rights groups. They worry that it may soon be possible to grow human body parts on animals. Patients with a worn-out part will then be able to have a new part grown to order. What do you think about that?

## Pigs that glow in the dark

In 2006 scientists in Taiwan created pigs that glow in the dark! They used **genes** from jellyfish to make the green glow. This was part of research into the treatment of human diseases. Green-glowing body cells could show up in a diseased part, helping doctors to keep a closer check on a patient's progress.

This genetically altered pig's snout glows green, rather than the normal pink.

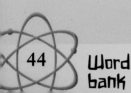

**Word bank**

frostbite  when body parts freeze, and may become damaged

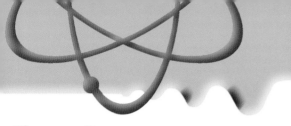

# Frozen for tomorrow

Scientists have not only worked on creating life, they have tried to beat death too. Is freezing people the answer? Some biologists consider freezing bodies, to bring them back in the future when they can be made healthy. After all, a frozen body can sometimes come back to life…

In 2001, one-year-old Erika Nordby crawled outside on an icy night in Edmonton, Canada. She froze to "death". Her toes were frozen together and her body "closed down", dropping to half its normal temperature. She was rushed to hospital after being frozen for more than three hours. Yet after an hour of treatment, her heart started beating again. Despite having **frostbite**, Erika recovered with no lasting brain damage.

## Can you believe it?

Scientists in the United States have already frozen hundreds of dead people in ultra-cold liquid **nitrogen**. The hope is that they will be brought back to life in the future, when medical science will be able to make them healthy again. The bodies are injected with a special human antifreeze and then kept at minus 196°C (minus 385°F). Don't try this at home!

Dr. Lemler, president of Alcor Life Extension Foundation, Arizona, USA stands in the cold storage bay where heads and bodies of about 50 people are frozen. The first dead person was frozen in 1967.

nitrogen  colourless, tasteless gas that makes up most of air and is very cold when liquid

# Biology in the news

Biologists have learned never to be surprised. Even though they know so much, they keep discovering amazing new forms of life on our planet.

In 2004 a new species of human was found. The remains of small people that lived only 13,000 years ago were discovered on the Indonesian island of Flores. The skulls and bones showed they were hardly half as high as people today. Peter Brown of the University of New England, Australia, made the discovery. He said: "The most remarkable thing is, there was a time when two very different human species walked the planet."

## Stop press – world's smallest fish!

In 2006 scientists discovered the world's smallest fish. Adult females are just 8 millimetres (0.3 inches) long, and the males are about 10 millimetres (0.4 inches). Biologists found the new mini-fish in forest swamps in Sumatra, Southeast Asia. The water there is naturally so acid that it kills most animals.

From the fossils found on Flores, scientists could tell that these small humans were just one metre (three feet) tall and had chimpanzee-sized brains – yet they made tools.

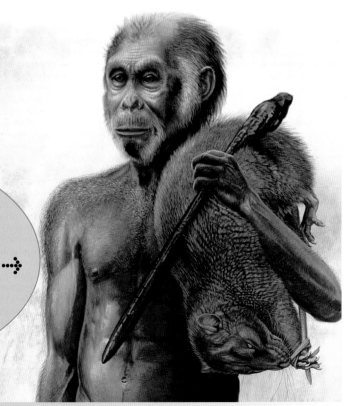

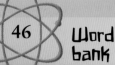

**Word bank**

suffocate  unable to breathe or suffering from lack of oxygen
tentacles  long flexible "arms" of some sea animals

## Giant squid

Marine biologists never know what they will encounter next in the deep oceans of the world. No giant squid has ever survived being caught, but some have been washed ashore dead. They had **tentacles** up to 18 metres (60 feet) long and a body two metres (six feet) across.

Then in 2005 a live giant squid was filmed in the wild for the first time. Japanese scientists took pictures of the squid 900 metres (3,000 feet) down in the ocean. As it struggled to swim away, it broke off one of its tentacles. This was still wriggling when it was lifted on to the boat. Biologists have the five-metre (16-foot) piece of tentacle to study.

### Mysteries of the deep

Biologists who have studied the washed-up bodies of giant squid found their blood does not carry oxygen very well in warm water. That could be why they keep to the deep, dark, cold ocean. A giant squid might **suffocate** in warm water near the surface. It could explain why these huge creatures are so rarely seen.

Giant squid are sometimes caught in deep trawl nets. Scientists suspect there may be an even bigger type of squid in the deep, known as the titanic squid.

## Wherever next?

Who can tell what biologists will do in the future? Many new projects would have seemed outrageous just a few years ago. Already biologists have changed the **genes** of plants, called **genetic** modification or **GM**, to make them grow differently. The aims are to produce crops that resist pests and diseases, to make fruit and vegetables that rot less and last longer, and to create crops that need less room to grow yet provide more food.

Some people worry that these new "science foods" could harm people who eat them. Others think GM crops will one day feed all the starving people in the world. Only time will tell.

## Can you believe it?

One day you may see a real live woolly mammoth! These great animals died out 10,000 years ago. But Japanese gene scientists hope to bring them back to life. By getting DNA from mammoth remains, and putting it into elephants, they hope to produce a creature that is almost nine-tenths mammoth within 50 years. How bizarre is that?!

You might be staring at a live woolly mammoth in the not too distant future. ···▶

**Word bank**

GM (genetic modification) altering genes by, for example, moving them from one living thing to another

## Tomorrow's world

Already scientists have developed ways to grow new body parts for ill people. Soon doctors may be able to remove liver **cells**, grow them in a **lab** and then plant them back into patients. Even new limbs could be grown in labs. If you need a replacement part, you may be able to order a new one and then have it fitted! In 2005 French doctors performed the first face transplant. They gave a new nose, chin, and lips to a woman savaged by a dog.

Whatever happens in the future, you can be certain that science will still be full of surprises. Biology will stay risky, and often weird … but never dull.

### The new hairstyle pill

Soon you may take a pill to change how you look. Scientists already say they know why hair grows straight or curly. They believe a pill could make your hair grow differently. Then people could make their curly hair straight, or change their straight hair to curly.

In November 2005 surgeons gave Isabelle Dinoire a new face. It was the first operation of its kind in the world.

# Biology timeline

| | |
|---|---|
| 3000 BC | Ancient Egyptians discover how to use **yeasts** to make bread, and how to stop dead bodies from rotting by preserving them as mummies |
| 350 BC | Aristotle attempts to classify animals into groups |
| AD 130–200 | Claudius Galen writes many books about the human body |
| 1628 | William Harvey publishes his book on the movement of the heart and how blood flows around the body |
| 1668 | Francesco Redi disproves **theories** of "spontaneous generation" using maggots |
| 1683 | Anton van Leeuwenhoek observes **bacteria** using his own microscope |
| 1760s | Lazzaro Spallanzani makes discoveries about digestion by experimenting on himself |
| 1771 | Joseph Priestley discovers that plants convert carbon dioxide into oxygen, a process called **photosynthesis,** as well as doing the opposite in **respiration** |
| 1780s | Luigi Galvani experiments with frogs and electricity |
| 1796 | Edward Jenner successfully **vaccinates** James Phipps against smallpox |
| 1859 | Charles Darwin publishes his book about **evolution,** *The Origin of the Species* |
| 1860s | Louis Pasteur explaines his germ theory of disease |
| 1865 | Gregor Mendel reports his experiments on the breeding of pea plants |

| | |
|---|---|
| 1883 | Robert Koch discovers the bacteria causing cholera |
| 1885 | Louis Pasteur injects his first patient against **rabies** |
| 1892 | Max von Pettenkofer drinks a test tube full of cholera bacteria |
| 1912 | The giant lizards called Komodo dragons are discovered in Indonesia |
| 1928 | The first **antibiotic** medical drug, penicillin, is discovered by Alexander Fleming |
| 1938 | A living coelacanth, long thought **extinct**, is found off the coast of Southern Africa |
| 1953 | James Watson and Francis Crick work out the shape of the **genetic** substance DNA, the "molecule of life", as a corkscrew-like double helix |
| 1996 | Dolly the sheep is the first **clone** of an adult mammal |
| 1998 | Scientists at Japan's Kinki University clone eight identical calves using cells taken from one adult cow |
| 2003 | The first version of the complete human genome – the full set of DNA – is published |
| 2003 | Genetic modification, **GM,** is used to produce a coffee bean that is naturally "decaffeinated", that is, it has none of the stimulant substance caffeine, which is normally present in coffee, tea, and similar drinks |
| 2004 | Little Nicky the kitten is the first cloned pet, produced at a cost of US$50,000 for a woman in Texas, USA, to replace her 17-year-old cat called Nicky, which died the year before |

# Find out more

## Time and the value of life

Wise words from a famous biologist:
"A man who dares to waste one hour of time has not discovered the value of life."
Charles Darwin.

## Using the Internet

Explore the Internet to find out more about the history of biology or to see pictures of famous biologists and their work.

You can use a search engine such as
**www.yahooligans.com**

Or ask a question at
**www.ask.com**

Type in key words such as

- bacteria
- Louis Pasteur
- penicillin
- respiration
- Charles Darwin
- DNA

You can find a lively introduction to the science of biology at
**www.biology4kids.com/**

There are facts and quizzes about bacteria, the microbes we love to hate, at
**www.nationalgeographic.com/ngkids/ 0010/bacteria/**

## Books

You can find out more about strange science and bizarre biology by looking at other books.

Arnold, Nick. *Horrible Science: Deadly Diseases* (Scholastic Books, 2000)

Arnold, Nick. *Horrible Science: Suffering Scientists* (Scholastic Books, 2000)

Townsend, John. *Incredible Creatures* series (Raintree, 2004)

Townsend, John. *A Painful History of Childhood: Nasty Bugs & Ghastly Medicine* (Raintree, 2006)

Townsend, John. *A Painful History of Medicine: Pox, Pus & Plague* (Raintree, 2005)

## Internet search tips

There are billions of pages on the Internet so it can be difficult to find exactly what you are looking for.

These search tips will help you find websites more quickly:

- Know exactly what you want to find out about first.
- Use two to six keywords in a search, putting the most important words first.
- Be precise. Only use names of people, places, or things.

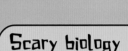

## Scary biology

In 2006 a Florida schoolgirl won a prize with a science project that proved water from the toilet is cleaner than the ice in fast-food restaurants! Twelve-year-old Jasmine Roberts visited five restaurants where she flushed each toilet once, then used sterile gloves to gather samples. She also collected ice from the restaurants to test at a lab. Jasmine said: "I found that 70 per cent of the time, the ice contains more bacteria than the fast-food restaurant's toilet water."

# Glossary

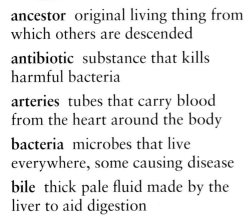

**ancestor** original living thing from which others are descended

**antibiotic** substance that kills harmful bacteria

**arteries** tubes that carry blood from the heart around the body

**bacteria** microbes that live everywhere, some causing disease

**bile** thick pale fluid made by the liver to aid digestion

**blight** plant disease caused by fungi or insects

**blood letting** cutting the body to let blood flow out

**cell** microscopic part or "building block" of a living thing

**clone** living thing that has the same genes as another

**crossbreed** breed together two varieties or species

**diarrhoea** runny bowel motions (excrement)

**Diplodocus** huge plant-eating dinosaur from 140 million years ago

**embryo** living thing in the very early stages of development

**epidemic** when a disease spreads quickly over a wide area

**evolution** when plants and animals alter gradually from parents to offspring over a very long time

**extinct** no longer existing or active

**frostbite** when body parts freeze, and may become damaged

**fungi** living things that feed on dead or rotting material

**gastric juice** powerful liquid made in the stomach wall to help digestion

**gauze** woven fabric of fine material or wires

**genes** instructions for features (like eye colour) which are passed from parents to offspring

**genetics** branch of biology that deals with how features are passed on, or inherited, from parents to offspring

**GM** (genetic modification) altering genes by, for example, moving them from one living thing to another

**habitat** natural environment or home of an animal or plant

**Hadrosaurus** duck-billed, plant-eating dinosaur from 80 million years ago

**hybrid** offspring of two different species or varieties

**laboratory** scientific work place for experiments, called a "lab"

**larvae** young, wingless, wormlike grubs

**mandrake** poisonous plant, whose root was used as a drug

**microbes** tiny living things only seen with a microscope

**mites** tiny spider-like animals that live on plants, animals, and stored foods

**nitrogen** colourless, tasteless gas which makes up most of air, and is very cold when liquid

**nutrient** substance that gives nourishment and strength

**phlegm** thick slime mucus in the nose, throat, and air tubes

**photosynthesis** when plants use light energy to make their own food, giving off oxygen in the process

**plaque** sticky film of old food and bacteria on teeth

**pneumonia** lung disease causing fever, cough, and wheezing

**pockmark** round scar left on the skin after a spot or blister

**predator** animal that kills and eats other animals

**pterosaur** extinct flying reptile with large wings

**pus** thick yellow or green liquid caused by infection

**rabies** deadly disease of the nerves and brain

**respiration** when living things take in oxygen and release carbon dioxide

**spore** tiny seed that can grow into a new mould or fungus

**suffocate** unable to breathe or suffering from lack of oxygen

**tentacles** long flexible "arms" of some sea animals

**theory** general idea to explain how something happens

**transfusion** putting fluid like blood from one body into another

**urine** waste liquid passed out of the body, usually pale yellow

**vaccine** dead or weakened microbes which make the body resistant to a disease

**virus** tiniest kind of disease-causing microbe

**vomiting** being sick or throwing up

**yeast** microbes called fungi that help to make some foods, including some types of bread

# Index